AF094892

I AM NOT CRAZY

I AM NOT CRAZY

I LOVE AND ACCEPT
MYSELF
THE WAY I AM

APRIL MIDDLETON

Xulon Press

Xulon Press
2301 Lucien Way #415
Maitland, FL 32751
407.339.4217
www.xulonpress.com

© 2018 by April Middleton

All rights reserved solely by the author. The author guarantees all contents are original and do not infringe upon the legal rights of any other person or work. No part of this book may be reproduced in any form without the permission of the author. The views expressed in this book are not necessarily those of the publisher.

Printed in the United States of America.

ISBN-13: 9781545642030

INTRODUCTION

This story chronicles the journey of Ariel Ruth Washington, as she stumbles upon a path of mental, physical, emotional, and spiritual healing. It is a tale of strength, about a woman who was weakened by trauma, abuse, and self-medication. Following recovery from a mental breakdown; Ariel attempts to overcome her past. Through journaling and self-reflection she is able to move on. Ariel recognizes that she is not the person who caused all the bad things that happened to her, and she is not crazy. She also learns that she must change the toxic relationship she has had with her own mother in order to move forward in life. While she is healing, Ariel clings to her faith and the love of her daughter to help see her through.

(I finished the entire book with good quotes (9-21-06)

9-8-06

I finally realized what it took me my whole life to understand. I may be my mother's keeper, but I AM NOT my mother. I am me & it hurts to feel like I'm killing her, but if that's what it takes to save myself then so be it. It is not crazy to leave your mother or move on with your life. It is however crazy to stay in the same place forever & never move up or down in your life.

9-7-06

What do you do when you think your life is falling apart & you think you are crazy and no one cares but you??? You save yourself and only then can you save the world.

A. Washington
(At the hospital 9-5-06 to 9-11-06) 6 days 5 nights

9-8-06

Mariah's (my little sister) birthday is coming up soon & the only present I can give her now is freedom. When she showed me the tattoo she had, I was jealous that I was never able to react to stress the same way.

When my mother had heart surgery & my dad was on heroin Mariah told the school I was her mother & her parents were dead. I just realized that wasn't crazy talk, because it was real to her. Now I understand it's real. The only names I can remember now are Rose, Ariel, Mariah, Jordy, Tania, Richard & Karen.

I always knew Karen would be the one to save me, I just didn't know when. Now I realize why I never lost her # or anything she ever gave me =) This whole time I thought I played a trick on the world, but now I realize the world played a trick on me & I'm ok with that!!!

9-8-06

That's why the only people capable of making me jealous are the six people on my list. They are <u>real</u>, or at least they are to me. My whole life I was always the one to ask why & the only problem was that I stopped asking why a long time ago. Everyone has a right to know why & no one should be ashamed of it, especially not me. I feel like finally for once, if I keep telling the truth something good will come out of it. I will be able to save <u>my</u> daughter Charlotte Rose Washington. That's the only date I can remember anyway & that's okay. I spent my whole life taking the blame for everything and everyone but it's not my fault. I didn't teach myself all of this mother you did. The <u>biggest</u> mistake you ever made was telling me the truth =) Now you can't hurt me anymore because my mind is free.

9-08-06

I feel like the meds are working except for the #2 bathroom scene. But since I told them the truth they treated it with Maalox. So I guess the only real treatment here is truth. The only time I tell the truth is when it is absolutely necessary. Truth, I never felt more alive than I did in this place. It's sad to say it took me coming to a psychiatric unit to realize I AM NOT CRAZY! Now I feel like I'm finally ready to leave this place, but I'll leave when they say I'm ready. After all Doctor knows best <u>right</u>!!! I feel like now I'm just biding my time until I return back to the world and to Rose. I do have a choice, I always have a choice; I choose <u>life</u>!!!

9-8-06

I guess I can relax now. I know it sounds silly, but when I came here, I believed my mother would come to kill me in my sleep even through these walls. The more I realize this is real, the more I know she's not coming for me. Hardest part to swallow is remembering her last words to me.

"I know I pushed you... I'll give you the money back I swear!" All I wanted her to say was I'm sorry Ariel, I know I was wrong!"

I always believed something was wrong with me, now I'm realizing something is wrong with them for being too selfish to save me. I resent my whole family except for Mariah, I just wish I could tell her that. And everyone else on my list. I feel like I'm gonna write till I'm blue in the face & not stop till I'm ready to leave my mind once more. The reality is I always knew I had the power.

9-08-06

I just didn't realize how great I was until being in this place. I really just realized my nervous breakdown was very necessary. Everyone <u>has</u> to lose their mind in order to get it back =) That's the God's honest truth =) =) I'm happy to say it!!!!! Now everything I didn't think I know, I realize I always knew. Like when I was in third grade & "fell off" the jungle gym and really "let go" of it cuz I wanted to know what is was like to die. Or the time I jumped in the left end of the pool & Uncle Abe had to save me. I wanted to die so someone would save me. I always wanted someone to save me. I just didn't know that someone would be me.

9-8-06

In our home on 8 Cherry Street things have been appearing and disappearing my whole life & I just now realized that was a problem!!! I feel like I really had to fall this hard in order to get my life right. It will be right one day, because I have Charlotte Rose Washington & that's all the strength I need.

The more I go over this in my head the more I realize I'm not a PATHOLOGICAL LIAR!!! I'm simply addicted to the one thing in the world I never had, "My Mother" Ms. Andrea Cole =) and there's absolutely nothing wrong with that. The first step to beating any addiction is to admit you have a problem. And I did that so now I am ready for whatever's next. First things first though, is a shower LOL =) =)

9-8-06

I finally let my hair down for the first time in a long time. I realize how beautiful I am and no one has to tell me that cuz I believe it now. This institution is <u>real</u>. The people are <u>real</u> and so am I!!! I guess that is the meaning of life. I feel like if I stop writing I'll somehow forget this horrific/wonderful experience. I know God is real. I was upset because I thought he abandoned me, but I <u>Knew</u> he didn't. Like the poem Footprints in The Sand. Amen to that one, Amen for <u>real</u>!!!

My footprints are in the sand.
I'm free thank you Lord
I will not be a victim.
I am a survivor
I will not walk in shame
I will not be intimidated
I never knew the poison
killing me was you. My past.
My set of footprints.
I will not abandon my friends
I will not be bullied
I'm going to remain good

*Anyone that will stay,
will stay. I tell the Lord,
Anyone that will go,
will go.
But I will not ever forget
Who I am, and where
I come from. Why, when
I needed someone
I was alone? Lord you know
I will not be denied my footprints
So you carried me through it.*

9-8-06

It's 6:15 and I know because I just looked at the clock. I'll shower in an hour and 15 min & I know that's for real. In here people tell the truth even when it hurts to hear it & I love it. They (the staff) don't just tell me what I want to hear. I realize now that I didn't ever trust <u>anyone</u>, cuz I always knew I was being used by the one person I could never please, my <u>MOTHER</u>!!! When my family would call me an alien from outer space or tell me I didn't belong <u>here</u> (there) I always believed them. Everything they did to me I did to Mariah that's cuz I knew she would be the one to set me free for taking care of her & everyone else. I remember her saying to me when I was having my <u>breakdown</u> "Everything will be alright Ariel. You didn't need to be the one to fix everything." I was so relieved when I made my escape the frightened, scared, shy Ariel told her "Please come with me downstairs, I grabbed my daughter, phone & ran like the wind (well walked fast as hell). I prayed the whole time if I'm not dying God please help me to know what's real & he did.

The more I sat up and felt like I was going through withdrawal, I was. It took meeting Suzie & everyone in the institution for me to come back to reality. Rose is reality & I won't ever do to her anything my "mother" did to me. No one should be made to feel that hurt or alone like I did that day in August my "brother's b-day" the day that I lost my mind. Now here it is a week later & I'm just now getting it back. That's some crazy shit!!! I can laugh at that now. This is real to me & I know it's real now because every time I think I'm falling, I remember to focus like the nice lady told me. I don't even care how I'm not wearing anything under this night gown or maybe my <u>paranoia</u> is actually going away. It feels like it or at least for right now & it might not ever go away. I'm ok with that because the treatment makes me feel better than I ever did in my life and that's the <u>truth</u>!!! I feel like I don't have to keep saving the world, cuz I finally saved myself. That's why I remember only what I want, because I always have. I'm ok with that now, because I did nothing wrong <u>mother</u> you did. Every time I tell the truth I feel guilty & lie. I didn't realize I was never part of you to begin with. You sick twisted sadistic witch. I may not be able to say this out loud but at least I can say it. I'm so tired, but I feel like this is the first time I really don't wanna sleep. Cuz I know something big is coming & I'm scared but I'm more anxious than anything to get it over with. Everyone has a voice, I just didn't realize I had lost mine until now. Now that I know that, I think I'll be okay. That my friend is the truth & nothing but the <u>truth</u> so help me God!!!!

9-8-06

I just realized whenever I get stressed, all I need to think about is Rose. All the paintings I did here when I couldn't remember anything at all that stayed consistently was/is my love for Charlotte Rose Washington. I feel like she's my guardian Angel & God sent her to save me. She was the only thing I really ever did on my own. So if I keep thinking about this it will stay forever in my mind, real!!!

9-8-06

Now I can say I don't hate Bush cuz when I go home Tania's gonna be there. I want a tattoo like Mariah. I want Rose to know her father like I never did. I don't want to lie to her even if it hurts. Once you start you'll never stop until you face your own mega beast "Mother." Everything keeps coming back to you. Now I'm ready to leave & I won't come back to you ever again. "Mother" I always knew you were just like me, you made me what you are. "Mother" I love you deeply for it now cuz you brought me here!!!

9-8-06

I'm feeling better now. If I write again it will be <u>real</u>. It is real I know that now. I'll do whatever it takes to get better to get back to Rose. Even when I feel I'm losing focus, I think about Rose. She is my salvation and I know that now. I don't ever wanna forget that again. No matter how hard it gets I just keep thinking about how it will feel to touch her & love her & teach her well. All I have to do is keep telling the truth & I can save her. I don't have to save the world anymore just myself.

9-8-06

I'm getting more restless by the second & I know something is coming. Something bigger than life itself, bigger than me.

They say I have a few more days however, I think today is the day!!! I have the same feeling that I had when I knew I was coming here. I'm missing Rose like crazy & that's okay. I'm gonna do everything in order to get my life & my daughter back. I think Suzie isn't crazy or anyone else in here.

It's more the people on the outside that are crazy. They can't deal with reality so they (my family) force their reality on me. It's always been this way, but not anymore. I'm gonna make a change & continue to change until my life is what I want it to be. Thank God for that one. I really mean it now!!!

9-8-06

I just found out Mommy tried to kill herself. I hate what I'm doing to her, but I can't go back on everything I'm trying to do to save her. I'm always trying to save her & that's what landed me in here 9-20-06!!! I'm so sad but excited at the same time & I don't feel guilty to say that. I'm glad Mariah & Rose are okay they are all I really care about & they know it. It's just so hard to feel the blame for things beyond my control. This is beyond my control now. I tried speaking to someone but even here they only listen when they want to & that's okay. I just wanna get out of here. I feel like I'm doing good but I can only do but so much & that's okay. I really do care about my mother. I'm just upset at the way I was treated & that's the gist of it.

9-9-06

Today I woke up missing mommy like crazy. The fact that she tried to kill herself made me more sad than angry. She always manages to turn everything into a "Poor Andrea" situation. But that's ok this is all about me and Rose. No matter what I can't forget that. I love her so much I'll take the pain in order to get her back eventually. And that's what it's all about. I kept saying I was ready to leave, but had she done this while I was home I would have been there instantly so I'm glad I was here & not home to save her. My life is mine & I know that now. Every day here is more like reinforcement of another day. That's ok with me because I will be ok eventually when they (staff) finds out what's wrong with me. Until then I need more shampoo, conditioner & deodorant in order to survive here. I'm not as scared as I was before & that is ok with me.

The fact that Uncle Vito (my dad) & Uncle Darryl came to see my mom pisses me off a lil, but I'm glad they couldn't come & convince me of anything otherwise. I'm glad that was the case. Now I can focus on myself and not everyone else.

9-10-06

The two Ariel thing makes me a lil confused. But I know she's real cuz I see her almost every day here. I just didn't pay attention to her name. The fact that she purposely hasn't had me makes me know she's been thinking about me and that's cool. I love the fact Rev Anderson, Mr. Eldridge, Mickie, Mariah, and Karen were all thinking about me. Now I'm thinking about me. I forget this book everywhere & remember it when I leave it so I know it's real. They finally have my meds right and that's real. I know it cuz I write it. The Maalox is real cuz I use the bathroom when I take it. Maybe hours later but I don't doubt it works. This is my diary cuz I write in it. After this day I'm not gonna stop until I can't write anymore. Maybe one day I will reunite with my mother, but not any day soon.

Not unless I have a fat chance with her in the hospital in Framingham on the psych unit. That's where she belongs cuz she did this to me & I did this to her & myself. I know that now. It doesn't make it right, but that's life. I'm so tired from walking back & forth. I'm about to go to sleep until Karen and the girls come. I won't forget Max, Gray, Ariel, Dr. Goldiehawn (even though I met him on the first day.) I won't see him before I leave but that's cool. (9-20-06) Dr. Frumpy is on call for him tomorrow. I have all the time in the world & I mean that now. Cuz this is real & so am I.

9-9-06

I met a lady who sounded just like me. She was older however she suffered a mental break like me. During group today I realized why I moved from alcohol to cigarettes to marijuana. I was trying to self-medicate instead of addressing the root of my problems. I realized I enjoy eating, sleeping & doing laundry only not when forced to. I enjoy letting someone take care of me for a change. We all make mistakes we just need to recognize that a problem exists. After this experience I'll recognize for the rest of my life that I'm mentally ill & there's nothing wrong with that =) Amen =)

9-9-06

I was told by a nurse Carrie that Karen's coming this afternoon. For some reason I believe her. Karen hasn't lied to me since she met me a few 3 yrs. ago. (9-20-06) Everything she said has come to pass. That's why I didn't lose her # or anything she has ever given me. I would just hide it from my mother. I didn't know I was doing it until now. Even with my meals I give away what I don't want and it feels good. This place has taught me how to live the right way & I know that now. When I'm sad I draw or write in my journal or go to sleep. When I get too weak to do much else, I go to sleep & that's okay. That's the normal thing to do & I know that now. Continuing everything I started here will be hard, but I have the greatest motivation of all. My daughter Charlotte Rose.

9-9-06

Today was a good day. I did everything I did on the first day I came here today. And the repetition felt good to me. Having a routine schedule worked out well for me. I didn't realize how much I enjoyed it, not having all the pressure on me for once felt good. Having people say you're a good kid & actually believing it was the best part. I think I'm gonna be okay after this experience. The <u>triggers</u> at the hospital saved my life & I know it now.

    Going to mass was fun even if I'm not Catholic. I miss Rev Anderson & the church a lot. When I get out that's one of the first things I'm gonna do, besides go to see Rose. I feel much better and I remember when Linda told me I'll be ok & Jorge and everyone else that knew they were leaving & I would eventually & so did I. I really do love this place like my mother, but I'm not ever coming back to her again. I do want to ask her why eventually but I'll get that chance one day.

9-10-06

As my time here comes to a close, I realize just how wonderful this experience keeps on getting better. The more I think I know the more I am taught here. My life was wrong before I came here & I see that now. But I'm gonna take a nap I'll holla back at you later Ariel =)

I'm back & feel really good. I just played bingo with Gladys & her husband Mann. It was really fun game. The sun is starting to set like the game we played with Ara. There's a new boy David here (9-20-06). He would be cute if I was at home and saw him. Well he is. Even the Jamaican guy that works here is decent looking. It makes me miss Richard even despite the way he treated me. I fell in love at first sight like Agnis did with my brother. Like I told Mickie I'm gonna reunite our family. I know it and I'm ok with it. I feel better than I did my entire life.

9-9-06

I'm not getting out today & that's okay with me. I just keep thinking about Rose & that makes all of this bearable. For some reason I thought everyone was lying to me in a good way but part of me knew they weren't. I called Rochelle to check on Rose & that made me feel better. I know this is for a reason. Even when Karen cried when she left I couldn't cry. Cuz I know everything will be alright will be alright eventually. I need to get my plan together but I'll do that in due time. I'm just gonna wait for the next activity. Until then sleep will be my best friend & I'm ok with that.

9-10-06

Max said yesterday really was my last day & I believe him & everyone else here. Even when I think they (staff) are lying, I know it's for a reason & that is to make me better. That's the ultimate goal in being here. I woke up today at 12:30 and eventually went back to sleep. I didn't realize that I had. I was happy today cuz I believed I was going home. I even remembered my different type of meds and what time. I felt good about that. I know I'm going home tomorrow & it's ok I forgot my towel & locked myself out of the bathroom cuz I told the truth. The doctor isn't taking my mind away like Katie always says. I know Max's my worker & Dr. Goldiehawn is my doctor here & that's ok with me. Amen to that & I mean it. I'm about to shoot for the stars & I'm ok with that.

9-10-06

I'm so happy I could scream. I know I'm getting out tomorrow talking to Mickie made me feel better. I was telling her the truth on the phone and she knows I'm ok. I was a bit upset Mariah called with the mommy bullshit, but I got over it cause I know she loves me. I know my mommy loves me too she just needs some help from upstairs, feel me. I'm not ever gonna stop writing again. I want that rematch with Gladys and her husband Mann. David is alright, but Speen is funny too. Everyone in here seems like all a part of me. I don't cringe when people are near me anymore. Even Derik I've gotten used to. I love Joyce's hair; I know I did it. Now I'm gonna call about Rose & if Rochelle doesn't answer supervisor it will be. Holla @ me youngin woo-woo!!!

(At Hospital 9-21-06)   *9-11-06*

I'm laughing at the fact that all my dates were wrong and I just realized it was September 11. I remember exactly where I was when it happened so I guess (I know) my mind is back. Getting out today is exciting & scary at the same time. I realize the plant job was imaginary. The clothes are damp because there is more than what I started with. I wiped my board clean & wrote on it after I felt better again. There are two Ariel's here & that's great cuz I can be me. I wanna do everything & nothing & I'm ok with that. Even if mommy finds me I'm ok with that too cuz I do love her. I'm just upset she was too selfish to help me & that's the truth =)

(Correct date when leaving 9-11-06)   9-21-06

I'm getting out today & it's because they (staff) finally know what's wrong with me. I've always known I just waited for someone to tell me. I really don't care what happens as long as Rochelle stays on her job & stops acting like I have all day every day to wait for her. That's why I don't trust her cuz I know she's in it for the money. (*Perception of mistrust transferred onto her*). That's why I couldn't cry in front of her. If I see Rose tomorrow I'll be alright. The time Karen plans is five and that's ok cuz I'm feigning for her bad. She's in most of my paintings & things here. I've noticed a lot in here that I didn't know I did until now. I feel ok cuz the medicine is working. I'm so anxious my blood's boiling & probably always will & that's fine by me.

(At Hospital 9-21-06)   *9-11-06*

I feel better knowing that Rochelle is doing her job. I don't resent Terry for thinking I'd be here longer, it took me 6 nights & 5 days to snap out of this and I know that. I do trust Karen for real because no matter what she doesn't lie to me. She doesn't ever tell me what I want to hear and that's a fact. Mariah called and I wasn't even mad at her for telling me that sick shit while I'm in the psychiatric unit. If my mom really cared she wouldn't be in a hospital like me she'd never stop trying to save me. I feel like she gave up a long time ago & used us children as a crutch in order to not deal with reality; The same thing I do with Rose. I don't want to do that anymore I want to live.

(At Hospital 9-21-06)   9-11-06

As I'm about to leave, I packed my bag & am ready to go. I've never been more ready for something my whole entire life. I'll say see yah like Rose does & Amen to that. Now I'll wait till they come & get me cuz I'm ready for it. I'll miss everyone cuz it's so bitter sweet, I almost wanna cry but I'm happy for real this time I am. I'm gonna do all I said I'll do in due time. Like my picture said one day at a time. So gimme one for the money doctor. I'm ready to live.

(At Home)

Now I'm home & I've never felt more free. I will get Rose back eventually, it will just take some time for me to do it. No more 9:00 bed time for me. I can do everything & nothing & I love it. I escaped finally I can save me.

My List   *9-11-06*

Get a psychiatrist ✓   *Dr Desarae for now*
Go to outpatient therapy 9-26-06 ✓   *1:00*
~~*AA get sponsor*~~ ✓   *Karen or Aggie*
Attend court   ✓
Get Rose ✓   *Starting to 9-20-06*
Job ✓   *lined up*
School   ✓
Dentist
Glasses/contacts
Keep taking meds
Place to live ✓   *for now*
License/car
Hair out ✓
Clothes/pj's ✓   *for now*
Get refill on meds ✓   *get another in one week*
All Rose's new stuff* ✓
Go back to church (Call 411 church) ✓   *in another week with Karen*
Get doctor ✓
Visit with Rose's worker Thursday 2 days
Tell doctor refill meds in 6 days every week
            508-370-3299
            443 messages
     Call Dana tomorrow 508-270-4006
       Call Carissa wed 27 4:00

9-12-06

I'm early & I'll catch the worm. I have 13 min. In the hospital I learned to count the minutes very well. It was part of a counting. I realize I need a lot more than I think I'll be alright though. Everything will be alright. I just need to stay consistent like Karen told me to. During my break she was the only one I listened to all the way. I only heard what she told me and I'm ok with that. I have 15 yrs to file my suit against my family. I'll take that time to learn how to live independently & I know that truth cuz I believe it =)

(Partial Program 9-20-06)

I'm on my way & remembered my meds before I left. I was only 3 min late or by their (staff) time 12 min early like Jacqueline does. It feels good to have someone to walk with all the time that's the fun part. I just saw the end of an accident and a worker from the institution so I do remember somethings after all. This music is soothing too!!!

(Karen's House- 9-20-06)   9-12-06

I'm here & it's alright. I'm still here & so God loves me. I'm sure I will be alright, for now and everything is going as planned. I plan on doing everything on my list and I know I will because the process has just begun. I keep writing so I will know this is all real. The cab ride & intake process to the partial program works for me. Karen is my only contact and that's OK with me. I know that cuz it all feels real. When she told me all I need to do I believed/believe her cuz Karen has never lied to me before so she won't start now. Everything feels very consistent now and I love that feeling of consistency. Like Karen said it will be alright for real for real!!!

(Partial Program 9-20-06)

We're about to start the program & I'm ready it's 9:15 & they're

9-12-06

(staff) are gonna come in and get me soon & I'm ok with that. I can listen to all these real <u>voices</u> and know for once I'm not making this up. I'm gonna meet with staff & I know that's alright. I have read/ agree with my contact that is real. The meeting made me feel better. I know my conversation was real & it will be tomorrow & everyday afterward.

<u>*Spirituality*</u>
<u>*Healing Response SELF*</u>   <u>*MIND*</u>
<u>*SPIRIT*</u>*-UALITY*
<u>*SELF*</u>*-QUALITY like oneself*
Self-hate doesn't exist
<u>*PERSON*</u>*-ALITY- ACTIONS/ BEHAVIOR/ATTITUDE*
Heal from <u>symptoms</u> – Exhaustion
Nothing to fight DIFFICULT CHANGE
Freud///Aristotle- watch young see how they tick
Basic flaw of only male MD's needed to change way of thinking
Freud FLAWED* DIED OF MOUTH CANCER/ COCAINE*
1 thing Theory of <u>Motivation</u>
Seek PLEASURE
SEEK Avoid Pain
ALWAYS BRING YOU WHEREVER YOU WHEREVER YOU GO

I can't be tired!!! I know that for real cuz I'm part sleeping/awake during this discussion, however wonderful it is. That helps. Stay with it Ariel you're doing fine. I'm still here!!!. I'm still here!!!

<u>PSYCHIATRY</u>- <u>BEHAVIORAL HEALTH</u>
<u>MEDICINE</u>- *changing way feel & action s have to change!!!*
<u>Negative mind</u> to <u>positive mind</u> *by behavior*
<u>Drinking analysis</u>- *learn/get drunk every night*
<u>AA/NA</u>-*Open to everyone to go even the <u>doctor</u> has <u>hope</u>*
You don't change behavior by thoughts. Change thoughts by behavior Payton 9-20-06

<u>JUST DO IT</u>
I don't hate myself!!! I love me!!!
<u>COMMUNITY: GROUP PEOPLE UNDERSTAND ALL PARTS OF WORLD TO <u>YOU</u></u>
<u>BEHAVE INTO FEELING DIFFERENT</u>

9-12-06

Every time my mind wanders I need to bring it back and pay attention.
　"Common sense is not as common at all!!!"
　　　　　Monroe/Pharmacist (9-20-06)

　　　　Bricks are heavier than feathers.
　　　　　　Dale

I enjoyed the program today. I feel like I'm being tricked into helping myself some more. Each day it will get a little easier for me as long as I believe it will. And I do believe it now. Everyone here is so nice, I can't believe they all have problems just like me & that works. I was forced to talk, but not really cuz I always have a choice in my life.

9-12-06

I LOVE MYSELF & ACCEPT MYSELF THE WAY I AM

Meeting Aggie was so cool I think I'm gonna cry. I never felt more apart of someone in my life. And the best friend's a Gemini like my Tania & I love it. I hope to see her again one day & I won't ever forget everything she told me or everyone here for that matter. I wanna do AA too whenever that's possible. I'm starting to feel better. It will be ok if I keep telling, myself that eventually I'll believe it. I'm so grateful for this experience I feel my life is finally changing for the better. And I'm ok with that for real... for now_____

I AM NOT CRAZY: I LOVE AND ACCEPT MYSELF THE WAY I AM

9-12-06

9-12-06

*ARIEL/ROSE DSS CASE
NEW WORKER CARISSA ALLEN
508-424-2500
Thursday morning 9:00 Court
Outpatient discharge papers*

9-12-06

Now I'm ready to sleep. I've never felt more ready than I do now. I will do everything necessary to get Rose back. She is on my mind all the time & I miss her like crazy but I know this is for a reason.

*Tomorrow I need to call <u>Regina</u>
And I need to call Rev Anderson and
No I didn't (9-20-06)

(At Karen's)   *9-13-06*

This morning I woke up early by an hour. Alana had cramps. I remember the feeling before I went to the psych rehab unit or as Colby says resting place. I'll get visits in a day hopefully. And I have court. I'm gonna try & do my hair by myself. Hopefully all goes well. I miss Mariah, maybe I'll call her & Rev Anderson and Aggie. I have to call Carissa and reschedule after court for the home visit oh well one more day won't kill me. I'm doing the right thing for <u>now.</u>

*   I need to make some connections my hair is a mess & my clothes are fitting the same. I'm a size 10 the size I always wanted to be. I miss my sweaters & playing with Rose. Looks like I'll have to go back after all. (Partial Program) I enjoy talking to Jacqueline she always relaxes my nerves. Her voice is cute & little. Jacob even makes me laugh. I'm scared of Kimani cuz he reminds me of Rose. (not anymore 9-26-06)*

*   I stay away from him though cuz I won't hurt him.*

(Waiting for cab Metrowest   9-20-06)

The whole family is great. I just wonder how they feel about me. This cab is late. I've been here since 8:04. Maybe I'm gonna be riding with Jim again. He's cool and I know it. He's always made me laugh. I can't talk about group but I'll show you.

(Partial Program)

LOL I'm feeling more like myself now. Looks like I'll be waiting a half an hour. I can't get Joy and Gladys out of my head. Gladys <u>wooded</u> me to lose in scrabble and Joy the clepto always made me laugh. Kelly I'll stay away from & mommy until my mind is stronger than the guilt. It's starting to be and I love it. The feeling of caring about myself is better than any feeling I've had in my whole entire life. Looks like my routine is about to change again. I just enjoy being able to walk and do normal things like that. I can't wait to see Aggie for the last time. I'll miss her when she leaves. I wish this cab will come.

(Karen's House)   9-13-06

It felt good being the first one to use the bathroom. I forgot my schedule at home & just remembered that. I have to remember laundry & cut off the lights rule. Karen pays for everything that's a change I need to get used to. The queen Bee has fallen, but it's a good thing I needed this rest badly.

(Metrowest Waiting For Cab)

Jim's here I'm glad. We can wait together until 8:45. The cab is always late he says but the time for real is 8:30.

I'm back again. My transportation screwed up but Liane took full responsibility for it. I'm glad she did so I can go to groups. It feels like my life depends on it. I don't wanna be a mess for court. I need my hair done & clothes to wear maybe Rev Anderson can help with that. We'll see. (*Didn't have to Karen helped with that*).

I'm in the program now. I'm enjoying myself here still!!!

(At Partial) Didn't face it* 9-13-06

I'm gonna have to face my big bad wolf today of all days. My dad died 6 days from now & I finally admitted that bothered me. I know my mom is sick & twisted and I'm scared, but Rev Anderson has to be with me. (*No he doesn't*) Then I'll go to AA/NA @ 7:00-9:00. I need to talk to Carissa before today is over though for real for now=)

I went #2 finally on my own. The fact that all my ailments are from stress & anxiety drives me up a wall. That is just not right LOL =) yet it is. Now I'm really doing everything I said I would.

Fill out registration form
9-14-06 10:30-5:30 → Court 9:00
Nov 14 only available appt
Waiting list

(At Karen's)

Thank God I don't really have to deal with my family. I just don't want to do anything & stifle my recovery. But thanks to Karen I can relax and do it all at my own speed. I did lose all my self-esteem, but now I'm gonna get it back. With her help I will do it like I said, even if it kills me. So now relax, no big bad wolf for me just yet =)

After shopping, I reinforced everything I knew. I'm still in withdrawal stages from my mom. I know she has pneumonia & I know she has a breathing tube but I'm ok with that. I'm just anxious to see Rose and feel her. Hopefully after tomorrow all will be well again. 9:00 is the time we'll see how court goes. I just pray to God all is well with me in their eyes.

9-14-06

I'll take all the necessary steps to get her back and that's fine. As long as I have help on my side we'll see where everything goes.

(At Karen's)

Today is my big day. I know it will work out fine. I haven't died yet so I can keep the faith. I'm kinda glad no family members will be there. I don't want to see them except Mariah (*No more Mariah*). I still love and miss her. I wish shell be alright but I gotta do what I gotta do for me & Rose regardless of the outcome. I hope & pray she transitions back to me smoothly as possible.

(At Court) 9-14-06

Today turned out great. I get to see Rose in 6 days and another visit in 11 days at the house. My next court date is Nov 13, 2006. I will have to bring Rose. I missed her a lot as we were shopping. Seeing Yari was cool I missed them too. I didn't know Mariah was that far off the mark. She'll never admit something's wrong anyway just like mom. I realize she is still under the influence of Andrea Cole and I'm not anymore. I'm glad I was not able to go to her or feel her "pain" so oh well. Maybe one day when her tears do not affect me, I will talk to her. Until then we'll see what happens with Massbay & work. Who knows where I'll be.

9-20-06 4:00 165 Fountain St
9-25-06 4:00 Home visit
11-13-06 9:00am Court

I LOVE AND ACCEPT MYSELF THE WAY I AM

Today I woke up on time. I didn't realize how tired I am. I probably won't get my PCP until next week but we'll see. Only five more days till I see Rose. I can feel her growing stronger every day. She has her shots and is in day care. They say I'll get her back in a few weeks under Karen's supervision. I'm gonna enjoy that. Their whole way of life is different and I like that. They all feed

9-15-06

off each other and not just one person and I like it. I realized I saw Raul the "crackhead" but he smiled like he knew I would be ok. Then a red car beeped at me and I couldn't remember what or who it was.

This is just a lesson to parents; if you are mentally ill then tell your kids about it. They'll find out one day when they contract that illness or they tell someone about your meds. I never knew there was a pill book that you can look up meds and their street names. If you have AIDS don't lie about it cuz you could be putting your whole family at risk, unless you tell them they can't help you. Like Stephanie yesterday, she would get off till she had extra credit and homework she had the night before. She won't be successful until she stops procrastinating. She'll catch up one day hopefully. I have hope the cab will be on time.

(Waiting For Cab)   *9-15-06*

Court went according to plan. I felt good telling the truth vs. lying. It's like I'm waking up from a bad dream. Yari was real and it was good to see her & Jose and tell my side of story. Mariah's not doing too good but she won't admit something's wrong. I knew she was lying. My mom still has a noose around her neck but I can't worry about that. I have Rose to worry about.

(Partial Program)   9-15-06

I'm here now and I'm alright. Reflecting on my days yesterday was good. I'm listening to everything more clearly now than I did before. I'm glad I came I missed everyone and knew it. Karen is teaching me how to live & get everything I ever wanted and I'm gonna do it all eventually.

(At Partial)   *9-15-06*

I didn't miss much. My meds are working so they say =) yes they are. I think I saw the culprit of our discussion last night before dinner. But being in a group makes everyone look less crazy & more normal. I feel more normal and like my parents & family are the crazy ones. I don't want to disappear anymore. I wanna live =) Watching the seat changes was interesting. I realize I really didn't miss much. I feel good all over. Everyone is starting to form groups but the dynamic will always change/evolve this way. Each person has a last day so we'll never be the exactly the same and I like it that way I feel I am learning just by sitting here.

Where there's life there's always hope.   *Monroe*

I wanna get my refill prescription if they find it for me. Probably by the end of the day. I notice they (staff) always watch us while we're on breaks. I know it, but does everyone else. I don't believe everything everyone tells me anymore. Pros & Cons are for everything.

9-15-06

I do want to leave here after I finish school. I don't want to always look over my shoulder with wonder like Colby said.

(At Partial)

Why is it I always go #2 when I'm here and not at home. Maybe because this is where my life started, so I feel most at ease here. This is where my life fell apart and came back together. I feel it all in this building, every time I come in here LOL =)

Today went by fast. I enjoyed the groups and realized I know everything that's going on. I knew the guy wasn't part of group or when I didn't get my prescription it was all part of a waiting game. I always feel like if I keep playing, the game will keep getting better. If I'm not here 2 weeks then great, but if so oh well what harm can it do.

9-15-06

Even in group I zipped through all the drawings, cuz I knew they were always there for me. This feels like everyone is really studying me & I like it. I feel important and I like that feeling too. I'm gonna go back to Massbay & work there. I'm gonna get Rose back eventually & I'm gonna marry Mark John Johnson III one day you'll see!!! I'm talking to the non-believer in my head, but I believe it so it's true & real!!! Like D'Ariel says for <u>now</u>!!! I think they're studying me the right way maybe something will come out of it.

9-15-06

Relaxation

Revitalize- renew- energy through the day (i.e. <u>walking</u>, write, read, shoot pool, swim. No artificial stimulants

<u>Guided imagery-</u> musical background with a voice guiding you through a scene
- *An alternative to be quiet with oneself*
- *Make time for oneself if for an hr*
- *<u>Meditation</u>- <u>Isolation</u> is a good thing ex. Anything involves becoming one with mind on your own.*

Experience inner spirit by breathing
1234 → breathe
*Central services in AA Boston
Friday night meeting
Temple shrine in Holliston

(At Partial)   9-15-06

Now that the day is almost over I'm happy that it is over (my group). So that's one day closer to my recovery. That word sounds good cuz I'm one day closer to seeing Rose. I won't let anything deter me from my resolve to get her back. Jim left early today so I waited with Megan. She's cool except she can't admit she wants a new husband. But I'm not here about that, I'm here to fix me. So I won't worry about the daggers they throw at me. That I throw at myself.

(At Karen's)   9-15-06

I realized that my mom has stalked me my whole life because she is a junkie. She pimped all her children to get high and never got any better. That's why I'm gonna stay the hell away from her & everyone associated with that life forever. I may not can run away from me, but I can run away from her. I remember my pact with God when I was 7 years old cuz I always tell Karen the truth, cuz she always told me the truth & I know it.

(At Karen's)   9-15-06

That's why I wouldn't sleep until Sean told me he takes the same meds as me for sleep. I take 100mg and I'm not that big so it works fast. I really don't sleep & that's me. But it feels good to know I'm not crazy.

I LOVE AND ACCEPT MYSELF THE WAY I AM

9-16-06

My weekend plan is pretty simple and attainable. I can do everything in any order and I will call Carissa before Sunday. I went to sleep on the couch cuz my thoughts caught up with me. I think I built up a tolerance for Seroquel, either that or it only works when I want it to!!! I can't wait for today to be over and all the next days until I see Rose at the office at 4:00 then at the house as well. Thanks to Karen I realized more about my life. Both my parents are and have always been junkies, that's why the drug dealers all got first dibs on us children in exchange for the goods. Mariah's doing bad & I know it but I can't save her only me & Rose sorry =)

9-16-06

Crazy
What do you do when you're life is falling apart
And you think you're going crazy and no one cares but you
You save yourself and only then can you save the world
They convinced you that you are a freak
But you are not crazy because they are
How can you ever save the world
I tell you
Save yourself first and the world will follow you
One day they will all follow you
Only then you realize you are not crazy
The world is crazy and there's
Nothing you can do about it

(At Karen's) 9-16-06

It seems like I've been writing that poem since the institution or "resting place" and I finally finished it. I had fun at the Jamn 94.5 thing even though I knew everyone there thought I was crazy. I really felt bad for Alissa's kids cuz they treated me the worst, but I still like all of them. I just don't like their ways. She didn't do anything. She knew if they hurt Kimani I wouldn't stand for it. He reminds me of Rose so much. Maybe one day she'll hear about her grandmother when she gets off drugs & really stays clean. I pray that day comes before she dies. I don't want her to but she will one day & I'm ok with that.

I LOVE AND ACCEPT MYSELF THE WAY I AM

9-17-06

Good morning I can write now. Both 1+2 were very good. I'm glad that I got to see those in a new light. I felt like I was Selen

Craven was my mother, Jordy was Lucien, Ben was Rose (Selen helped create him—make him a hybrid).

William was my grandmother Eliza Ruth Battle, and Marcus was Karen, Jesus was Victor's daughter and Victor was God. I feel like I had to kill my old perception of God in order to become the future (i.e. Selen). That's why I was happy when Karen (Marcus) killed (Kraven) my mother for me in real life by not letting her get me. I have to let the old Karen die in order to see her for what she really is the angel (Ben) or Rose!!! She brought me out of it, now I'm me again and I can become the future (Selen).

(At Karen's)   9-17-06

The performance was great. Too bad I'm not gonna be able to do the voice lessons. I wish I had known people before I asked and got my hopes up that it cost 30$. That's just a reminder of what I don't have. It's not my fault however; all I can do is focus on the future.

As for when I get steady on my feet, I will afford all of the things that I want. I'm proud of the girls being so brave and going for their dreams while they can do something about it. One day Rose will go somewhere like that where she can hone the skills God has already given her. Like Raquel and Matthew my cousins. I miss Raquel every time I see a performance of the arts I think of them. I remember at the funeral for Bee Bee everyone was talking about Matthew's girlfriend and her beauty. I didn't see her, so I felt guilty for leaving to take my mom to dialysis & leaving Rose with the family. I didn't think Mickie & them would hurt her, I just was scared that someone else would get to have a piece of her greatness!!! One day I'm gonna be great like her. I already am!!!

(At Karen's)   *9-17-06*

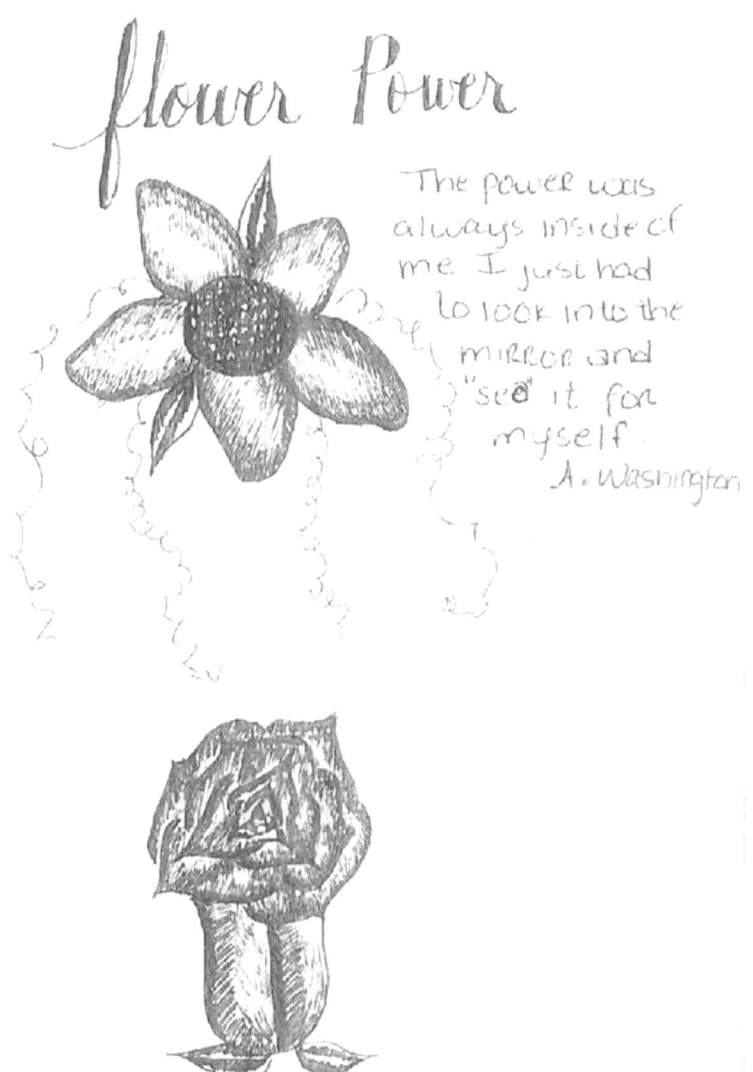

I am an artist

                       A. Washington 9-21-06

(At Karen's)   *9-18-06*

Today I woke up feeling good. I didn't know where Karen was so I didn't panic. She appeared to me last night when I woke up at 10:11 watching the seventh sign with Demi Moore. All these movies feel different this time around. My time of the month has been here 2 days and 3 nights for me. I knew it was coming Friday night. I did everything I could do on my list for the weekend so I feel great about that. I can't wait for the group to begin and go schedule my appointment for my doctor today. And I need to register for my PCP today after group.

(At Metrowest)   *9-19-06*

I'm waiting for Jim and the cramps are finally here. Since I left the house they crept up on me. I hate being a woman. But if I didn't have cramps, I wouldn't have Rose so I take that back. I can't wait for this day to start. I'm 2 days closer or should I say 2 nights and 1 day closer to seeing Rose again. She's so smart I'm sure she learned everything by now. I want to be like Karen when I get older.

9-19-06

I want to be scared but fearless; Frail but stronger and talkative so much I know it was all real. But there was nothing I could do then; so I'm making up for it by saving my baby Charlotte Rose Washington.

Group was alright today. Everything that I expected it to be. The gum Hanna gave me is spearmint & it tastes like spearmint. Randy is new and there's another Marilyn. I remember her from the first day (the other) Marilyn showed me around and bought the rest of my food for me. I was so thankful that she bought it for me so I wasn't reminded of everything my mother took from me. Including the 2000$ the last time I left. She has taught me a lot of good things as well but she should have told me she was mentally ill & had AIDS the truth for real. I won't believe anything she says unless I see it for myself. Her lies followed me all the way here.

(At Partial)   *9-19-06*

<u>*Self-awareness*</u> : *Understanding opportunities and limitations*
- *Knowing who you are- identity*
- *How you feel about <u>yourself</u> doesn't change based upon societies idea of <u>you</u>*
- *Consistency/ confidence*
- *Core values; sense of self*
- *Knowing personality & actions around others*
- *Skills, talents, attributes*

<u>*Self-esteem*</u>: *acceptance of oneself*
- *Self-esteem—win wars fight adversity*
- *High self-esteem -- value oneself love oneself*

The day is almost over & I'm somewhat sad. I didn't get my appt for my psych evaluation which I need but one day the timings will match up. I feel better than I did when I went to sleep. If I would have known about Partial I would have don't it a long time ago. I realize my mother has done the same thing cuz she's sick like me. I'm ok with that now. I can breathe again and know it's for real for now!!! Like D'Ariel says.

(At Partial) 9-19-06

I just went over my list from the hospital and realized I've done about everything on my list. That makes me feel great & like my accomplishments are real. I feel more real now than I ever did. Now my life isn't sin or a lie, and I love it. The sun is shining and it feels so good to end the summer off with a bang like this. The groups were fulfilling & I love the feeling of knowing I'm doing good and no one can stop me.

(At Neighborhood Health) 9-19-06

I'm at the doctor now. The walk was great. I feel like the sun never shined brighter than right now. All the events of my life lead me to here. There's no place I'd rather be than right here and now. My walk made me feel more protected than ever since I knew I was being followed the whole way. One of the perks of being on the other side now. When I close my eyes, I look forward to sleep now more than ever. I wish I would've known then what I know now I wouldn't have ever went back home.

617-784-3256 Aunt Nicki
617-913-7289 Anaia
October 11 2:45 Doctor's appointment

I LOVE AND ACCEPT MYSELF THE WAY I AM

(At Metrowest Cab)   9-19-06

Saw my Aunt Nicki this morning, she looked good. Everyone is here to be with my mom & I love it. They can't hound me. I'm glad my mom DOES NOT have AIDS & that's one thing gone from my mind. She also gave me 10$. I spent 1.78$ so I have 8$. That's a start. I'm glad everyone knows that my mom is mentally ill. I've always known and she knows it. I love her but I'm gonna still stay away from her until my mind is strong enough to face her. Maybe one day but it's not today. I feel better knowing she's getting better but it doesn't slow my resolve to get Rose and & be with her the way I want to. I'm not sorry she (my mom) tried to take her life that's a sin & I want no part of that life anymore. It feels great to say it and mean it. I can't wait to begin my life all over from scratch. I'm ready for it for once, for now_____.

(At Partial)   9-19-06

DISORDERS	SPIRITUALITY	HEALING BEHAVIORS
Complicated	Self- Quality	To see self accurately
Chronic	Self- sense	Use energy carefully
Difficult to identify	Self Talk	Healthy
(common symptoms)	(+) Give Self Credit	Self-ishness
Confusing	(-) Unduly harsh	NO!
Create stress/anxiety		
(+/-)		
Fatigue		

Doctor's Orders Desarae
Take all Risperdal at night with Seroquel
Take Atenolol the same time daily

I realized my issues with food started at home. I became obese when I drank soda (like my mother). Now that I'm me, my weight has not gone up or down. I'm smaller than I was in high school and I know that. I can fit into a size 10 and haven't been that small since grade school. I wanna know what made my weight change like that and why I couldn't talk about my older sister Kelly molesting/raping me as child? Maybe one day I'll get the answer.

(At Partial) 9-19-06

Anger Management

- *Problem when it happens <u>too</u> <u>often</u>*
- *Intense anger is never good *(i.e. call names, impulsive behavior)*
- *Crying is not too intense unless hurting expressions are being produced *(i.e. screaming over doing chores)*
- *When anger lasts too long it interferes with work/engagement of life*
- *Taking time out is not suppressing your anger (i.e. not negative)*
- *Postponing expression of anger*
- *How not to get angry at all (deal with it head on) *(i.e. self-talk, write a letter, fill in the blank)*
- *Become expert on oneself → anger *(i.e. identify what makes me angry)*

(At Social Security)   *9-19-06*

I'm at social security I have a bad pen

(At Karen's)   *9-20-06*

I slept so good I don't -didn't know where I was. Then I woke up & realized it was all real & I told the truth. I love that even in my babbling there's some truth to it. Thanks to my intellect and humor, this is all going according to my plan for my independence. I was selfless my whole life now I want to be selfish & there's nothing wrong with that. It feels great to have that notion reinforced by medically trained professionals. To know I have back up that sides with everything I've been saying my whole life makes me feel safe <u>for now</u>.

(At Metrowest Cab)   *9-21-06*

I'm waiting for the cab & Jim now. It seems to come right on time. I'm glad I'm always early so I can catch the worm. They say I have nice handwriting and drawing skills. That's like Peter Pan in a way. I never wanna grow old & I won't or at least not in my mind. I wanna be able to relate to Rose forever or until I can't anymore.

9-21-06

The break we had was long enough I don't want another till she goes to camp or college. Whatever comes first I'll be happy with. I miss her so much I'm so anxious to see her. I pray she remembers me and doesn't hate me. I don't hate/haven't forgotten her. One day I'll explain this all to her & she'll know all this really happened. I'm not gonna forget the time when I lost my mind and got it back. I saved myself and that's all there is to it (*God saved me*)!!!

(At Partial)   *9-21-06*

I'm at the program now. The ride I did with the cop was great. I didn't know he was one until he told us. I'm glad he knows my story and not what my mom told him. She stopped telling the truth a long time ago. She couldn't accept the fact she let the best thing in her life slip away, by not telling the truth and not letting me go. She tried to live through me so long eventually she wanted to become me & she couldn't admit that.

9-21-06

She tried to drive me crazy and I didn't know it. I'm so glad I went crazy now I can save me and Rose for real!!!

9-21-06

By the time I go to therapy I will remember everything I've held in my whole life. My mother did kill her mother. My mother's father and her mother met in this institution. The only mistake they made was telling the truth to their children like my mother told me. When we moved onto 8 Cherry Street she knew it was the house my mom grew up in that's why Mr. Karlie let her move back in. She killed her mother in 8 Cherry Street and I know that now. (*DISTORTED REALITY MY MIND TRYING TO MAKE SENSE NOT TRUE*).

I realize my mother has always been mentally ill and it's part hereditary. If she would have told the truth & kept telling it, I wouldn't be here realizing I'M SANE. I thank her for driving everyone crazy around her for me to realize she is mentally ill & she knew it but didn't want to go back here.

9-21-06

All our family has come here. The only people that moved on were those that admitted something was wrong with 8 Cherry Street. I'm glad I don't live there anymore. I'm glad that I live at 360 Walpole Street and I will be ok to sit here with my thoughts. I know I am not crazy. I'm still angry but that will go away one day. I just have to hold it together. I will make it right with the people that I wronged for real. I have to make my life right in order to move on. One day I will tell my daughter where she came from, and she'll believe me because I wrote it all down and I haven't stopped writing in this book. Because I don't ever want to forget what brought me here in the first place. I know she is not I, and I am not she, she is my mother. I think the more I keep telling myself I'm ok, the more I know I've always told the truth. We moved out of Boston because I never stopped telling the truth. I told DSS on my mom, I tried to die when I fell off the jungle gym when I was in third grade.

9-21-06

I jumped into the pool at 6 feet deep. I always wanted to die because I could not save my mother and I have to accept that. I love feeling selfish and know I'm this close to finding my salvation, which came in the form of a 6 lb. 15 ½ oz. 20 ¼ inch long little light skinned girl named Charlotte Rose Washington. I won't ever forget that because I remember today.

(At Partial)   9-21-06

Relapse

- *You have to get better to get sick again*
- *No specific time for recovery*
- *Autobiography in five short chapters III Portia Nelson*
- *I walk down the same street there is a deep hole in the sidewalk I still fall in… it's a habit*

My eyes are open I know where I am
It is my fault I get out immediately

(At Partial)   *9-21-06*

4 Stages of Denial/Addiction

1. Denial of the illness
2. Denial of help (I.e. I can handle this on my own)
3. Denial of treatment (I.e. willing to get help but not do life changes to stay)
4. Acceptance (I.e. know what changes are/will make changes to stay well)

-Healthy anxiety is better than overconfidence - Perry

This is the last time I'll write in this book but it won't be the last book I write in. I'm finally ready to leave this place and I know I beat my addiction for now for real. I know I am not my mother. I am Ariel Ruth Washington granddaughter of Justin Washington, Eliza Ruth Battle and Emily Mae Washington. I will never go away or disappear. I'll only get better cuz my mother never did.

(At Karen's)   *9-21-06*

My aunt Nicki told me my grandfather is mentally ill. She gave me 10$ after. I felt like it was a bribe to see my mother. I'm glad I didn't take it. That would be going back on everything I learned in group. I loved the meeting today I will go back and not stop. I can't wait for tomorrow even though I know what's coming. Yesterday was great. I saw Rose and I started in the community watch program. To think I picked up all the sexual assault pamphlets and the fact that they (Dr. Dans, Mrs. Hall & Mr. Walkman) sent Karen to me when I was seventeen makes me love them all the more. The fact that I went to her myself speaks for itself. I know I said yesterday was it, but I'm not gonna stop until I finish this book. I won't finish until I go to outpatient therapy in five days. I realized with Karen's help that I'm still trapped in a 7 yr. old body. I hated my mom when she wouldn't let me get double promoted & I told her. And she tried to kill me (strangle me) then cried & said she was sorry.

(At Karen's)   *9-21-06*

I think she always knew she was sick & couldn't handle the thought of death so she skated through the rest of her life being everything like me. She's beyond saving at this point. All I'm thinking about is me and Rose.

(At Metrowest Cab)   *9-21-06*

I'm waiting for the cab, I just realized Jim isn't coming anymore. When he finally told me he was 51 I realized he was telling the truth. Jim wasn't even his name and he finally told me the truth about that. I think he was a cop too! He never got charged a fair, I noticed. Either he's on a case or he's retired like the cab driver the other day. I couldn't believe my mom had lied again. I wish she wasn't always in denial. We could've talked about some issues. Like Kelly (my older sister) raping me as a child and making me give her oral sex. Oral sex is sex that's why Mickie left, cuz she & her mom knew something was wrong with that. That's why everyone hates my mom; she's been in denial since my dad died. She found the worst bad guy of all Willis P. Warner. If that's really his name, it is, but I always wanted to call him Willis, now I can.

I AM NOT CRAZY: I LOVE AND ACCEPT MYSELF THE WAY I AM

(At Partial)   9-22-06

Even here today everything gets easier every day. I can't wait for the group on relationships to begin. Pat's here so there we go.

<u>WHAT DOESN'T WORK</u>
<u>No Binge Healing</u>
*(i.e. keeping secrets)
TAKES TIME &
True expectations
Toxic connections
(i.e. people places things my family)
Impatience
Fear (Poison of our culture drives people)

Forget/**F**uck
Everything
And
Run

<u>ADDICTIONS</u> Eat your self-esteem (i.e. Fear)

<u>PRACTICAL Connections RELATIONSHIPS TIME</u>= Perception (i.e. idea)
<u>SAVE TIME</u>
        ALL
    Not real

<u>NO!!!
Patient</u>
Waits to heal
(i.e. patience)

Ariel = sign for Aries means Hope
My name means Hope

<u>WHAT DOES</u>
Make time for it!
LABOR SAVING DEVICES (i.e. microwave, cell phone)
Healthy <u>connections</u> (i.e. Karen, partial) AA/NA
Give self-time to heal
Stay free spirit (Take the fear away by <u>healthy actions</u>)
Accepting that we all make mistakes
<u>SELF TALK</u>
(know where to get help i.e. partial AA/NA)

<u>SELF ESTEEM</u>
takes away addictions when it is high (i.e. courage) Say No!!!

(At Partial)   9-22-06

I learned today that I can control negative self-talk. I can say no to everyone and no one and that's okay. I found forty feelings based on my attributes the more I realized it was all in my head. I added a Ness and Ality to the end of all the things that I think I am. I am my own worst enemy and I know that now.

I just realized I can watch other people eat. I'm scared to look at them & scared for them to look at me. Justin (my brother) called me fat & ever since then I never wanted to eat again. I always feel guilty about eating as well. I don't think there's anything wrong with that. I feel like I might have a cognitive distortion on my body image. I'm always gonna be the 185-200lbs pregnant girl or the fat girl all because my whole family is overweight. I don't wanna be sick to lose weight. I did it the right way unlike my mother. I realized I was mad at Brady for peeing on the floor when he couldn't control his bladder. But I can't control Jorge going to the bathroom after I take a poop cuz poop is real cuz I eat and when you eat you poop.

(At Partial)   *9-22-06*

I realized I'm guaranteed to eat, sleep, and shit & I'm ok with that. I am strong. I changed the water before Bill had a chance to when I could've told him and let him do it. I'm coming back cuz I wanna do everything again & that's ok as long as I still continue to save myself first.

(At Karen's)   *9-22-06*

I realize my mother is a junkie & I don't want to marry a junkie. I don't want to attract a junkie. I wanna talk. Maybe I do need AA/NA after all even though my addiction is a person. I will try not to go back into relapse even if it kills me. It hasn't killed me yet so I know I actually do have a shot!!! I can save Charlotte Rose Washington. I just have to keep telling myself that. I'm excited about AA I always wanted to go and speak before an audience. This might quell my fear of speaking in front of people. I noticed I still retreat when there is tension. I still don't like yelling but it's normal & I have to get used to it. I'm proud at the fact I asked for something I wanted & I got it.

That's my greatest accomplishment being able to speak up for myself and I like that I am becoming my own person after all. Thanks to Karen & this house for real. I'm gonna be sad to leave it but I know I will have to one day, but I don't ever really want to. I hope I haven't upset her too much however; the groups keep urging me to go to AA/NA. My addiction (*to my mother*) is real and I need help, so I'll start there. See you in a few hours.

(At Partial) 9-22-06

Last night was a success for me. I used the self-talk & write a letter method with Karen. She ended up letting me go to AA. I walked down there early. I need the 12 steps & stayed for a few minutes. When I got this itch that wouldn't go away I finally couldn't take it and left. It was not so bad but it wasn't for me. I knew I didn't belong and so did they. When the car pulled up in Dunkin Donuts I walked even faster to my home (360 Walpole Street). I cleaned up very fast in the kitchen and almost burned the house down &

I AM NOT CRAZY: I LOVE AND ACCEPT MYSELF THE WAY I AM

(At Partial)   9-22-06

I broke a dish but they all still loved me & I loved them. I realized I might not ever know if Uncle Vito is my dad and Bee Bee is my brother, but I'm ok with that. Maybe my dad was Justin Cole & he did die while we were children. Either way I am as much a Cole as Andrea M and even more so. (*UNCLE V NOT MY FATHER JUST A FANTASY DUE TO THE CLOSENESS IN RELATIONSHIP. MALE HERO FIGURE*).

I feel better after talking to John. I might go to a meeting tonight next to the police station. I don't think I'm gonna go back after that. I wanna keep the light in my eyes. I don't want it to go away. I feel better now that I have met a girl just like me. I realized we are all the same. Everyone is searching for something. I think I found what I was searching for here. I found my hope and faith again. I pray that I won't ever lose it again. I know one thing that won't ever change is my love for Charlotte Rose Washington. She still needs me and I'm gonna save her.

(At Partial)   9-22-06

PHYSICAL	MIND	SPIRIT
Walk	Yoga	Religion
(Exercise)	Meditation	CHURCH
SLEEP	+ Self talk	CHARITY
DIET (i.e. eat well no caffeine)	Breathe	(help us feel better)
Water 64 oz./day	Taichi Pets	Connection to greater
Vitamins (i.e. B-complex)	DIVERSION (i.e. reading, writing, tv, singing)	Nature (i.e. fishing in the lake)
Fish oil	TALK	
DANCE	Ask for help	

Can't solve the problem with the same mind that created it

(At Karen's)   9-23-06

Appt @ Massbay
9-29-06 Friday 10:00am
Eye exam
9-28-06 3:30pm 167 Union Ave
Contacts
10-04-06 9:30am 44 Union Ave (*bring prescription)

(At Karen's)   *9-23-06*

I got screwed up today, all I saw on the envelope was Regina's name and voices against violence & Karen thought it was for me. I saw 360 Walpole Street when it really said Harvard Street. I don't know if they're giving me Rose back but if they do I will be eternally grateful. I'll feel like I have more of a purpose again. If Carissa approves of the house, then I will be able to have home visits here & that's better than at the office. I'll feel more alive again.

   I'm sick from eating the hot dog and fries. I know the germs from the grill got me sick. If I drink enough water & take some medicine I will get better. The medicine (Robitussin) feels like it's working. It still tastes as nasty as it did when I was a kid. But they say what doesn't kill you makes you stronger. I must be hella strong, cuz I'm still here despite my crazy family's attempts.

(At Karen's)   *9-24-06*

Last night was fun. I played rummy 500 with Jacqueline for most of the night. She got really good at the game very fast. I think she is like the queen of rummy now. I'm glad I was able to pass my crown to someone as worthy as her. Today I'll try finishing True North. The book is good. It reminds me of me. Aeon Flux & Just My Luck were good too. I realized I only have to talk to my therapist now and that's cool.

I can't believe the scene Mariah put on. I think the reality finally set in to everyone that I'm gone. Andrea Cole cannot have me or my daughter to live off anymore. She wanted all my money so it's gone. She had my whole life to tell the truth and all she did was lie. If they come near me again I will call the police on everyone in 8 Cherry Street. I'm so glad Rose wasn't around for this. I have to stop letting them get to me like this. That's all Andrea Cole wants is a scene. I'll give her one in Framingham District Court. She'll have her day like she told me I'll have mine.

(At Metrowest Cab)   *9-25-06*

I woke up feeling good this morning. This old lady stayed in my ear the whole way but she didn't come in the hospital. I'm ok, I liked the smell of the guy that walked ahead of me as well. Now I have to wait for the cab so I can go to my second to last day @ Partial. I'm gonna miss that place. I found myself there. I found my voice there. I want to be a psychologist so I can truly know why I am the way I am. (*I ALWAYS KNEW*).

(At Partial)   *9-25-06*

I can't wait for the water machine to be filled. My mouth is dry. But I've grown used to hurry up and wait syndrome. I've had that my whole life. What's one more day. I'm sad but I'm ready to go. I've been waiting for this my whole life. One day I'll live and make it, look back on all this and think of it as a bad dream.

I still can't watch people eat. I'll probably never get over my brother Justin calling me fat as a child. I will always the 185 lb. fat girl for the rest of my life. But how do I change my perception of self?

(At Partial)   *9-25-06*

So that I am Ariel. I've always turned to or away from food as my comfort. The fact that the girl who called the people who robbed her house crackheads then admitted she was one made all the sense in the world to me. She's really smart & I could be her.

That's what Uncle Vito meant when he said one day it could be me. Everyone knew who I was living with. That's why I always felt guilty about leaving Rose at home cuz I really didn't ever know what was going on at home. The fact that I always knew floors me. It was when she (my mother) left me to get high. When I was 3 or 4 yrs old & I got lead poisoning as a child & she never told me why. She knew what she was doing & always lied to cover up the truth.

SHAME
Guilt (i.e. ashamed of leaving family)
Self inflicted

TERRIBLE		-Attached to actions
DISGRACED		& behavior
"LESS THAN"	GUILT	-How others
Hurt	SHAME	make you feel
Sad		Hard to change
Self-Pity		over the years
Embarrassment		
Resentment		Keep to oneself
Anger		(tired headaches,
Depressed		pain, nausea)
Defensive		
Lost		I _am_ the mistake
Anxious		I _made_ a mistake
Disgusted		
Confusion	MIND	-If ones affected all of it
Dirty	BODY	has chemistry upset
Helpless	SPIRIT	
Vulnerable		
Failure		
Abandoned		
Blamed		Fear of being seen for
Betrayed	Shame:	what & who we are
Rejected		attached to actions by
Alone *Isolated*		perpetrator
Silence		
Secrets		(VICTIM BLAMING)

(At Karen's)   *9-25-06*

I can't wait for tomorrow to come. I'll see what Karen meant by the whole house falling apart. I feel so weird without her here now. The phone visit went well. I'm glad I nor Rose, do not have to go back to 8 Cherry Street anytime within the near future. I'm glad my mom is still in the hospital where she can't hurt me ever again. I really do miss Karen I feel so lost without her. But she'll be back before we know it. I just have to keep telling myself that.

Tomorrow I'm gonna call Carissa @ 9:30 and ask her what the policy and procedure is on a parent <u>VOLUNTARILY</u> giving up their rights. At the hospital I was treated like criminal. They had me sign papers without any representation or explanation. There was no doctor with me when I signed the papers at the hospital. I'm not a child anymore & I'm not gonna act like one anymore. I'm gonna start asking why. (*ACTIONS OF PROFESSIONALS WERE TO PROTECT MY DAUGHTER, UNABLE TO SEE IT BEFORE*).

(At Metrowest Cab)   *9-26-06*

I'm ready for this day & my cab. This is gonna be a long day that I'm sure of. I'm ready to see Rose tomorrow. I don't want to be a fool anymore. Today I'm gonna start asking the questions I never asked before. Now I really do wanna know why and there's nothing wrong with that. Today's my last day at Partial and I'm ready to go but I am sad to leave all my friends. Like in the book True North. Lucy & Africa are one in the same but both are fighting for freedom in different ways. I think they're gonna find it eventually like I'm finding my truth now.

(At Partial)   *9-26-06*

I'm ready to end this and start a new chapter in my life. Now time for the next group, so I'll see you later. It's been 10 days into the program, and I'm ready to leave this place. Finally, I realized I am free. I can finish something & I know that now. I hope I don't ever forget. I found my truth here. I found me; Ariel Ruth Washington.

(At Partial)   *9-26-06*

<u>Healing</u>	<u>SPIRITUALITY</u>	<u>See Self</u>
<u>From what</u>?	<u>Self-Quality</u>	Through our
<u>Disorder(s)</u>	Increase in fear	own <u>feelings</u>
Symptoms	Feeling Powerless	MANAGE
Reaction		
<u>EMOTIONAL</u>	What you	
<u>Denial</u>	really <u>know</u>	**F**orget
<u>Distract</u>		**E**verything
<u>Conflict</u>	+ <u>Use It</u>	**A**nd
<u>Fear</u>		**R**un ⟶ <u>Action</u>
<u>Isolate</u>		

Finished

(At Karen's)   *9-27-06*

I am so glad I filed the restraining order on my mother. She's the one I'm gunning for. I did admit @ therapy for the intake I do want to kill all the lies with her mentally & physically. I feel like I'm free and I got my swagger back. Now I'm gonna keep it. I'm also glad I finished partial so I can finish everything else that I started.

                                                                    9-28-06

I can't wait to see if I get an apartment. I want to furnish it on my own. I pray my mom & the rest of the family get the hint & leave me alone and Rose too. Her foster mom Ara seems pretty cool. I won't do to her what mom did to me. She screwed me up but I'm still unscrewing myself now!!!

   The Rock came again today when I left. That reaffirms the fact I aint waiting for any celebrity. After 5 hrs. that's my limit. I'm not angry, I just know I can't wait for anyone that long. I'm not impatient, I just have limits. They end somewhere between 3 hrs. and 4 hrs. I'm tired and ready for bed. I'll see Carissa tomorrow.

9-29-08

I'll see what happens again tonight. I'm not too hopeful this time but the Rock is here until Monday. However, after today if I don't get an autograph I'm not going back. I have another visit with Rose in 3 days. I can't wait to see her and maybe show her a signature of the Rock. We'll see but for now I'll try to conserve my energy.

9-30-06

I finally met the Rock and got a signature! He went by us the first time & me and Kimani sat and waited. When he came back by I hoisted him up with one hand and stuck my hand out with the other. All I could muster to say is "please". I know he heard it. I felt him scribbling on the paper and I knew he was signing it. I'll save it for Rose so one day she'll know all my life's new changes were based on her. This metamorphosis was motivated by Charlotte Rose Washington.

10-01-06

It's raining today. I did three drawings. I was proud of them. I can't wait to do the show at the library. I have a lot of work to choose from. I also can't wait to see Rose tomorrow at 9:30. She's definitely well worth the wait. I can't wait to have her back permanently. I know I did the right thing giving her up to protect her & I will continue to do so!!!

(At Home Karen's)   *5-31-08*

It has been a long time since I have written. A lot has changed since then. My old journal has weathered and worn some of the most life altering moments in my existence, and I survived. I am a graduate of Massbay. It feels surprisingly great to say that! However, I am a junior at Framingham State College as well. If all goes well I will have everything set by September. On June 4, 2008 God willing I will get my license & get a car hopefully. Rose is growing to be such a beautiful young girl. Now it seems Mr. Leonard has had some big epiphany. Why is it when men are incarcerated they find religion

I AM NOT CRAZY: I LOVE AND ACCEPT MYSELF THE WAY I AM

(At Home Karen's)   *5-31-08*

ethics and empowerment??? He is shouting for the world to see she is mine and it has not been confirmed. I will give him credit for accepting his responsibilities, but it is just a little too late =(I can't ever go back to being less than nothing. I love myself and my daughter entirely too much to subject ourselves to that sense of nothingness. Today was great!!! Charlie picked me up at nine am and we bought entirely too much food & other items. Karen and Peter were a little early & George was extremely early as well. I had to run around a million places and came back to find Mrs. Joan Purry at the door. Jasmin was the next to arrive. Jeremiah came shortly afterward & Harley Rae made the most fantastic spinach and rice casserole. Mell brought apple pie + ice cream my favorite combo. Even Veronica came bearing gifts. I made over 100$ profit for the day. It was small + intimate like I liked and am comfortable with. The small groups made me feel special because I knew they cared. Their presence even for 5 minutes showed me volumes on their character.

(At Home Karen's)   *6-5-08*

I finally have my license some 5 yrs after high school! It seems everything that could possibly go wrong did go wrong, but finally I have arrived. Too bad I pledged my first paycheck and savings towards my laptop. I have to start from scratch but it will all work itself out in the end. I'm so elated I can hardly breathe. I definitely believe coming to Karen's was the best decision I ever made in my whole entire life. I've excelled more in the last two years than in my entire existence. Everything happens for reason and it seems life is going according to God's ultimate plan. I realize it all worked out the way it was supposed to in the end. I will definitely remember this day. When I let go and let God there was a coming together for everything to just be.

(At Home Karen's)   6-9-08

Rose had her first date with the dentist today. She did surprisingly well. She only cried a little bit and wouldn't go do the x-rays, other than that she was great. I got my free whitening trays

(At Home Karen's)   6-9-08

today which was awesome. There are a few issues on my mind today. First every time I do something individuals feel entitled to every aspect of it. It seems like all my life, people feel entitled to what I do which floors me. Also if you are reprimanding someone you feel the need to let everyone know and give "play by play" when you know I heard you. That is hilarious to contemplate. I had lunch with a blast from the past. She cleared things up royally. But I must distance myself from everyone like I've been doing. It worked. Even her with her good intentions; a little too bitter for me. I guess I will never have a real friend again. I must accept that. It seems no one (from the past) is at the same place in their life as me.

Those that are could be my parents and often switch between the roles and it irritates the heck out of me. On another note all of this heat will help me lose some weight which is kinda cool. I just really need a car. Then a job to maintain it. I also need to clear some things up. There will be no more public speaking engagements for me.

6-9-08

I've conquered my fears and I would like to be done with it. These whitening trays feel weird, but it was free so I definitely cannot complain. Thank you Lord for everything. I know I am blessed =)

(At Home Karen's)   *6-12-08*

I received my license in the mail today. It looked so different and the letters were blue instead of red which was pretty cool =) Colby fixed the shower for now!!! Who knows how long it will last. I just keep playing the waiting game to see how things are going to play out. Not just here but everywhere and every aspect of my life. On the one hand the stability was great but on the other hand sometimes it's like suffocating, choking the life outta me with restrictions. There are so many things beyond my control, and at the same time, I am just feeling my way through it all. I'm enjoying different parts of the new job. It is weird how I always end up in a beneficial situation on both ends. I guess I've got a lot of "angels" looking out for me. Thank God they did otherwise Lord knows...

(At Home Karen's)   *6-14-08*

All is coming along. Maybe not as well as I'd like, but it is really quite amazing. Today we saw Maria and her granddaughters and Rose remembered them and Katrina from turns out Maria's mother. Isn't it a small world. I saw Danny when I went shopping and I feel so grateful for being myself again and Rose being who she is. Even seeing Caldin today at Dunkin Donuts was alright I didn't pretend not to see him. I just waited until he approached and stayed very calm! It was surreal almost. It seems old habits die hard with some. Like Russel Simmons says in his book, the wrong people for you will bring you down even if it's not intentional. So just smile and keep it moving and no worries for you. I am definitely glad to be where I am. Thank you Lord.

(At Home Karen's)   *6-16-08*

It is uncanny how quickly the tables turn. People will allow themselves to be dependent yet instruct others to practice independence. As the chips fall where they may I am getting to a content place in my heart. I will however not take unwarranted negativity to protect others anymore. People need to take responsibility for their actions. When you actively choose to wait until the last moment to prepare then try to switch the focus that falls on you. Sorry for you!!! Those that forget time waits for no man have a rude awakening when you realize the world will not be waiting on you hand and foot. I know I will not play the victim nor will I allow anyone to place me in that situation anymore no matter what. It's extremely funny how others react when they cannot manipulate you. Then everyone scrambles to find out who to blame. But I realize it is no one's fault just human nature. I am the master of my destiny. Thank God for my new awakening. I feel so alive more than I ever have in my whole life. I feel so cleansed in my soul =)

(At Home Karen's)   *6-18-08*

My therapist returned from Ireland and helped me shine the light once more. I find myself looking forward to our biweekly visits. I cannot wait until Friday to get our cd's I ordered online for me and Rose as well as the laptop I got for school. It seems like after all that other issues arrived in my life. It feels good to see everything finally coming together. I'll take baby steps like I have been. I will get to a higher place eventually. I finally finished my Russell Simmons book. It flowed so well and every time I had added anxiety there was a subsequent page with the right message. The relevancy couldn't come at a better time. God has some strange plan that it isn't exactly one set the way you would like or plan for things to be. I don't think we even quite figure it out completely but I guess that is the beauty in living.

(At Home Karen's)   *6-23-08*

Today was a very productive day for me professionally and personally. I finally have everything set for my laptop, it will be here 10 days after my 23rd birthday. Thank the Lord =) As well, I got call backs for the agency's I was seeking out and completed one task out of 3 assigned by Skip =) I think the company sees me as a valuable asset and they are definitely rolling on all my terms. I've been blessed I must say. They provided transportation, increased my hours, gave me a desk, phone, business cards, and put my name on the website to name a few. I even was able to revise my title after request. I am eternally grateful to say all the chips are slowly falling into place. The only negative is trying to balance all of the different things. I feel that one side always feels slightly rejected and it is not what I want at all. I need to find a way to balance or bring the issues to light, one way or another things aren't working properly anymore. I just pray for God to lead in what is the best way to deal with my life. My #1 priority is Rose. I thank God she is healthy.

(At Home Karen's)   *6-29-08*

Well it seems all will be revealed in due time. I'm conflicted in the sense that I can't take road one or two, but each way results in something being left behind. I don't want to exclude anyone and it has become inherently clear that both sides are considering what they will lose versus how I will ultimately be affected by the culmination of the two worlds. (*STRUGGLING TO DETERMINE HOW TO MAINTAIN SECRET CONTACT WITH "FAMILY" AND OPEN CONTACT WITH MY NEW FAMILY*). Some go out of their way to cause conflict to bring to light hidden secrets, yet I face the truth alone. Unfortunately, where I'm headed will probably be less stress and better managed solo without distraction from either side. I'm letting God take the lead here at this point. I'm not quite sure what the outcome will be.

For anyone who has experienced trials and tribulations on this journey called life, just know that you are not alone.

www.ingramcontent.com/pod-product-compliance
Lightning Source LLC
LaVergne TN
LVHW041711060526
838201LV00043B/676

I AM NOT CRAZY

April Middleton is a licensed mental health counselor. She received her Masters of Arts in Psychology with a concentration in Couples and Family Therapy. April is bilingual fluent in English and Spanish. She specializes in trauma treatment providing individual, family, and couples therapy. April enjoys working with underserved populations within the community which has been a passion since childhood.

Las 4000 PALABRAS MÁS usadas en INGLÉS